A Path Towards Pregnancy

Musings of 2023

poems by

Aarron Sholar

Finishing Line Press
Georgetown, Kentucky

A Path Towards Pregnancy

Musings of 2023

ACKNOWLEDGMENTS

The person who I have to thank the most is my fiancé. Together we made a decision to create a family, and together we struggled through all the humps we had to deal with in the process. Thank you also to my parents and friends, who were always excited for this journey I went through. This project was inspired by Victoria Chang's *OBIT*, as I wanted my own work to be raw and real just like hers. I thank her greatly for this inspiration. Finally, pieces from this chapbook have appeared in *JAKE the Mag* (2023) and *In Parenthesis* (2023).

Publisher: Leah Huete de Maines
Editor: Christen Kincaid
Cover Art: Kelsey Limpert
Author Photo: Aarron Sholar
Cover Design: Elizabeth Maines McCleavy

Order online: www.finishinglinepress.com
also available on amazon.com

Author inquiries and mail orders:
Finishing Line Press
PO Box 1626
Georgetown, Kentucky 40324
USA

Contents

For my future child

We read to know we are not alone,

a wooden-framed chalkboard sign on the wall reads. On the way to this bookstore is when I first said *I am considering having a baby myself* to these people I considered friends, but we were really just school friends. But I told this car full of friends this truth I'd never even spoken to myself. In the bookstore, a friend calls *hey Aarron, come here!* And I wander to her. In that car, I remember the words pregnancy, uncomfortable, desire—and the book she shows me is on just that: *transgender pregnancy*. I recognize the cover, of the two men standing with their three children, two taken-on and one produced, because this is the book I'd ordered off Amazon only a week prior. I put it back and take another lap around the bookstore. An hour later, on the way out, I go back to the book, bring it to the counter, and pay an expected small-bookstore-price for it. I put this copy away in my desk, to be kept safe—until I have the idea to take it out again and give it to my boyfriend. And I do; *look, we could have a baby like them.*

January

On the day before the New Year my uterus clenches itself as I walk into the work bathroom. I open the cabinet door for a pain pill and am met with examples of tampons I will learn to use in the coming months. I take note of Her, the uterus's, pain, because She's my focus for the coming year. I am going to see my boyfriend an hour and a half away tonight because this year She will start to bleed and clench Herself every month, and soon she will house a tiny life inside of her as my brain tells Her *no we are a man we are not supposed to want to hold life here* but she will respond *it's my duty* and I agree with her because when I look into this Minnesotan's blue eyes I want to create a child with those same eyes.

February

When I visit my boyfriend one weekend, I cry when I don't want to cry. I cry because the first time we have sex that day, he cannot finish and then it is my turn to house the inability. I cry because even after trying all my sex toys for twenty minutes, he has that look in his eyes that make me cry, the look of boredom. That's when She froze, unable to feel pleasure for the rest of the day, and She begins to feel pain after he thrusts a dildo in too deep. I don't tell him She's in pain and this time I don't take ibuprofen to relieve Her anger. I let her wallow in it.

March

In the call center I work at, we take death calls. When someone dies, we take the information and give it to funeral directors. Today I get a fetal demise. 17 weeks. I Google how big the fetus would be; only a pomegranate baby. One day I too will have a pomegranate baby. I *want* a pomegranate baby. What if mine also breaks open, seeds spilling out inside of me and then my insides spilling out of Her? I prepare my body, letting it reset after six years of testosterone, and it already bleeds as it did in high school. If my future pomegranate baby breaks open, I'll bleed then too. There's always blood. If I lose the pomegranate, there will be tears. I brought the blood upon Her again, will make her carry out the fertilization she was designed to do, all while my brain is actually my pomegranate baby. That pomegranate baby is already, will continue to be, broken. Everything is broken; my mind, the pomegranate, Her. The only unbroken is on the outside, on the nights when She bleeds, as my boyfriend wraps his arms around me and warms Her with his hands.

April

A lot more of me is broken now. I convince myself I'm depressed– due to the upcoming graduation and the academic exhaustion? due to my brain chemicals changing because of the lack of testosterone? due to an actual depression setting in? I am working on my issues with intimacy, but the other week, I again cried when my boyfriend wouldn't eat me out. I cried because I got my period, and She bled, so he didn't want to, and I wouldn't let him either. Another day, we simply have no time. He probably doesn't because he just doesn't, but I sure want him to. I want him to devour me like he hasn't eaten all day, but when he doesn't I cry. First I cry because of this, and now I cry alone in my own bed because I try to make sense of why I can barely do the last schoolwork I plan to ever do, why getting up in the morning is a chore, why this video game I am playing bores me within minutes. *Oh well, another item to discuss with my therapist this week.* By the morning, I am feeling better. I report that I didn't get my period to the app on my iPhone, and it tells me my fertile window, when I will ovulate, and She will bleed next. I hope for the day I move in with my boyfriend, so during that fertile window, we can try. Until then, I'll stay in my bed, cry a bit, and imagine my weighted blanket is his body, embracing me in his warmth.

May

Our friends have a baby who turns two in August. The baby and his mother are at my graduation party and I see a hint of the father in my now fiancé. The baby sits on his lap, the large man-sized hands wrapping around the small torso. He lifts the baby up and flips him upside down, a laugh erupting from the small lips. After a few flips, the baby is done and wanders off. The next day, She begins her monthly ritual. I go to change the tampon that has been inside her for only two hours and there is no white. Some chunks of internal flesh cling to the bloodied white– the blood drips from the tampon onto my fingers. I sit on the toilet for a moment, nothing in Her, just to know for a moment what it feels like to be unburdened by my body. But as I sit on that toilet, I think of those man hands around the baby torso, and I decide I can handle the chunks– for my, our, own baby.

June

My therapist tells me I'm no less of a man because I get a period– want to have a baby. But I am. When I sit on the cold men's room toilet at work, I am strategic. Men don't expect the crackling opening of a tampon. There's no box to put its remnants in. I open the stall door once I'm finished, ready to chuck the used fluff and wrapper in the garbage immediately, but a real man walks past me into another stall and I freeze. *Did he see my hands?* Men don't have babies, women do. I am biologically a woman, and I want to have a baby. When I see my fiancé play with our friend's baby, I feel Her tense. She wants one, I want one, we want one. I am less of a man, but I also feel the energy of a mother. A mother-father. How can I be a mother-father? What *is* a mother-father? My therapist tells me I'm no less of a man because I get a period– but what am I?

July

Maybe you should try a dog first– babies are expensive ya know– those things take a lot of work– is all I hear when I report to my new coworkers that I can't wait to have a baby. Always the negatives: time, money, effort. No, I don't want to try a dog. I'd rather get a cat anyways. I know babies are expensive, but the two of us make 100k a year, so I think we'll be fine. Who doesn't expect a lot of work with a baby? Heck, even trying for a baby is a lot of work. I want to put in the effort, to deal with the adorable handful, to look at a pregnancy test and take to Amazon's 2-day shipping for a shirt that says *I love hot dads* and wear it until my fiancé notices and then he'll realize we've done it. I want to see it pay off. I want to spend money on a crib, changing table, highchair, play pen. I want our town house to be decorated in baby items and the corresponding giggles. I want all this, and no, I *don't* want to try a dog first.

August

I sit down at my desk and my head hurts and my chest hurts and I am nauseous. I took birth control at 1:45pm and I know I can't be pregnant but for a millisecond I ask myself *what do I do if I get pregnant and I'm not actually ready?* Our friend who already has a baby says you're never really ready but I have a dream that a doctor tells me I'm pregnant and I'm not excited. Dream me isn't as excited as I should've been. Dream me doesn't want to go through with it– Dream me wants to abort the fetus and now real me is wondering if I really want to have a baby so soon but at the same time I wonder if I want a vaginal birth or a c-section. I look up pictures of c-section scars while staring down to my own– self harm, accidental, mastectomy, *c-section? Birth? Producing an adorable little life with the man I love?* I think I can handle one more scar.

September

*Thank god the test is negative. Sweating all day and waiting for 5pm so I could pop into Target on my way home. It was so sweet how he offered to buy me a test too. But no, it's my body and I'll pay for whatever care it needs. I tell him the same thing when it comes to tampons and pads. Three minutes is suddenly the longest wait ever. I watch the timer and the test at the same time. A single line, phew. But why are my eyes tearing up thirty minutes later? He comes home at 9pm and I know I need to talk with him about this. Maybe I **do** want to start trying for a baby now, as I'm just getting my footing as an adult. I'm only 25, do I need to have a baby so young? But my body is back to its natural cycle and is running as normal and I had to plan six months in advance and it's now or in another year because I'm at the point where I need to get pregnant or go back on hormones and if I start hormones again then the schedule resets. Another six months. He'll come home tonight, eat his leftover pizza, and ask how my day was. I'll tell him about my sweating all day with anxiety and hoped every bathroom break there was blood between my legs and the worry is all gone when I got home and saw that single line but then I cried because there was only a single line but I wanted there to be two.*

October

She hasn't been cramping, and so right before I leave for a job interview, I lay the stick on the bathroom counter. I watch the urine cover the window that I assume will show me everything I've seen before—that single line. I go get dressed, pulling up my black jeans that are quite tight now. I watch my hips sit on top of the waist of the pants. I look like a muffin top. I'm disgusted, turning away from the mirror to button up my favorite dress shirt. The shirt is tucked in, the collar secure. I glance down to the test, and I'm frozen. I walk in a small circle in the bathroom until I can pick the test up. Two lines—I'm an incubator now. I go buy that *I love hot dads* shirt as soon as I am done with the interview. My fiancé tells me that at this point, the thing is no larger than a single grain of rice. I look down to my stomach, I press on Her just slightly, and I swear I could almost feel that little rice grain within me. My body is suddenly not just mine, but ours. But—

November

—the first ultrasound does not show the expected. Inside my body sits a sack, *the placenta* the doctor tells me. There is no kidney bean, no heartbeat to listen to. The being hides. She, my uterus, holds this being—a being that may be life or may be a sack. I stare at the Once Upon a Child sign across the street, the colorful letters attracting their key demographic. Some strollers sit outside, somehow untouched by the elements, waiting for a birthed being to wiggle its way out every five minutes. I want to set my being in that stroller. But they're not for sacks.

December

My pomegranate baby never made it to a pomegranate. I had a blueberry baby. A blueberry sack. I stare into the toilet, the thing obscured by bright red. The figure was a silver dollar pancake—flat and almost circular. I stare at it. My body broke. My body broke and it broke this pancake or blueberry or sack or whatever it is. Blood. Tears. One in four. I think about the other *whatevers* that were broken—blueberries, pancakes, pomegranates, watermelons. My pancake wriggles with the water before it is sucked away. I crawl back into bed, and my fiancé wraps his arms around me with a small snore.

We ███ **know we are** ████████

████████
███ this ████ is when I ██ said I *am*
having a baby ████████
████████
██████ this truth I'd █████ spoken to myself. ██
                                                                                              I
wander ██████ I remember █████ *pregnancy*,
█████ *desire*—and the book she shows me is on just
██ *transgender* ██████ I recognize █████████
███████████████████████████████ one
produced, because this is the ████████
████████
██████████████ way ██ I ██
████ bring ████████ and pay an expected ██
████ price for ████████
████████
████████████████████████ *a baby* ██
██████

Aarron Sholar, author of *A Path Towards Pregnancy: Musings of 2023* (2025) and *The Body of a Frog: A Memoir on Self-Loathing, Self-Love, and Transgender Pregnancy* (2024), has had works published in *Reckon Review, WORDPEACE, Stoneboat Literary Journal, Tangled Locks, Prose Online, Thin Air Online, The McNeese Review, The Broadkill Review, Sierra Nevada Review,* and more. His essays have also been nominated for The Pushcart Prize and Best of the Net. He holds an MFA from MSU, Mankato and a BA from Salisbury University. You can interact with him on Twitter/X @aarron_sholar and at aarrontsholarwriting.wordpress.com.

www.ingramcontent.com/pod-product-compliance
Lightning Source LLC
Chambersburg PA
CBHW022110080426
42734CB00009B/1551